A QUICK GUIDE TO
e-LEARNING

A QUICK GUIDE TO
e-LEARNING

A "how to" guide for organizations implementing e-learning

Gregory C. Sales, Ph.D.

Andover,
Minnesota

ISBN 1-931945-02-0

Library of Congress Catalog Number: 2002091592

Printed in the United States of America

First Printing: April 2002

06 05 04 03 02   6 5 4 3 2 1

Expert Publishing, Inc.
14314 Thrush Street NW,
Andover, MN 55304-3330
1-877-755-4966
www.expertpublishing.com

*Andover,
Minnesota*

*Seward Learning Systems, Inc.
www.SewardLS.com
612-721-4444*

for Michael and Christy

Contents

ACKNOWLEDGEMENTS

Few publications can be attributed to one individual. This one certainly can't be. The information I provide here has been influenced over many years by other authors, colleagues, students, staff, and clients. I truly value the input, both formal and informal, I received from all of them. I thank them for helping me to better understand the learning process and the application of technology in promoting learning.

Specifically, as it related to the preparation of this book, I would like to thank Heidi Sonsteby-Naughton for her assistance in editing the content and Frank DeMars for preparing the figures.

INTRODUCTION

As I look back upon my two-and-a-half decades working in the field of e-learning, I can see that my passion for e-learning has steadily increased. Why? I believe it can be attributed to the field itself: changing understandings of how people learn, new development tools for the industry, new delivery technologies for e-learning products, and increasing interest from an expanding array of organizations hoping to benefit from e-learning. These things, and the challenges presented by each new project, make every day a new and exciting experience for me.

This book contains information of importance to executives, training directors and managers, and e-learning team members. As an executive considering an e-learning strategy for your organization, you will be exposed to issues important to your decision making. Topics addressing everything from Learning Management Systems (LMS) to Return on Investment (ROI) are presented and discussed. As a training manager or director, you will benefit from the discussions on approaches to specific problem resolutions and the models to guide the design of your own solutions. As a development team member, you will benefit from comparing my approach to e-learning design and development to your own.

The reason for my brief treatment of the topics in this book is simple. Your time is precious. What I endeavor to do is provide quick access to information that will help you do your job. Each of the chapters in this book is worthy of a semester-long graduate-level course. I distilled the information covered and, where appropriate, related it to models in an effort to make the larger process clear.

The models and processes I describe provide a solid foundation from which to work. Using them, you can confidently begin to build custom e-learning solutions for your organization.

I encourage you to contact me if you have questions, concerns or comments about e-learning in general or this book in particular.

Greg Sales
gsales@sewardls.com

Section One

This section consists of four chapters. In these chapters I provide you with a basic introduction to e-learning and the related terms and concepts you must understand to meaningfully discuss the topic. I define and review e-learning, provide real world examples to illustrate the range of e-learning products, and explain foundational concepts, team structure, and project hierarchies.

1

What Is
e-Learning?

The term "e-learning" is a relatively new, and somewhat trendy term, that means different things to different people. Like "e-mail," "e-business," "e-commerce," and a host of other terms, "e-learning" has only recently become a part of our lexicon. Obviously, we need to have a common understanding of its meaning. To that end, I provide the following brief definition of e-learning, followed by several e-learning examples:

> *e-learning—the use of electronic technology to deliver education and training applications, monitor learner performance, and report learner progress.*

Let's examine that definition more closely.

First, the phrase "electronic technology" literally means "computers," and could be any of the following:

- A stand-alone workstation that runs a program off the hard drive (see the laptop scenario).
- A networked computer that runs a lesson from a CD-ROM (see the LAN scenario).
- A pocket computer, connected through a wireless network, which runs a lesson from an organization's intranet (see the PDA scenario).
- Any of a number of other computer configurations.

Second, the phrase "education and training applications" refers to the activities designed to move learners through a structured series of experiences (such as lessons), with the goal of achieving specific learning outcomes (such as measurable knowledge gain in a content area or observable changes in behavior). These experiences may be wholly or partially online.

Note that e-learning excludes electronic postings, such as online manuals that someone may read and study. Instead, posting information of this type is often referred to as "information dissemination." It lacks the structure needed to guide a learner to achieving specific learning outcomes.

MONITORING PERFORMANCE

Depending on the needs of an organization, e-learning software *may monitor learner performance* in very general or specific ways. Examples of monitoring learner performance include tracking the following:

- When the learner finishes the training.
- How long it took the learner to finish the training.
- The number of correct responses a learner makes.
- The percentage of correct responses a learner makes associated with specific learning objectives.

Let's face it: Accountability is on the rise in most organizations. The capability of e-learning to document participation and report each learner's progress makes it an exceptionally appealing training mode. Because of the role of the computer in e-learning, it is possible to track literally everything learners do—or don't do—in a lesson.

One caution, however, save and report only information that is important and will be analyzed by someone within your organization. Collecting too much information can be a burden to the system and training managers. In some situations, it may suffice to have the software simply report progress in a lesson to the learner.

CONFIGURATION SCENARIOS

The following scenarios illustrate the range of e-learning training activities. These will broaden your understanding of the variety of hardware and software configurations that can be used to deliver education and training.

Laptop Scenario

You are a new sales representative. Your company offers a new hire training program for many employees. But the costs associated with bringing you to headquarters for training, and the need to have you in the field selling products, mean that you cannot attend.

As a part of the initial orientation provided by your field supervisor, you are provided with a laptop computer. This computer is integral to your work. It contains tools you will need to do your job successfully, such as product presentation programs, online manuals, pricing tools, and order processing programs.

To help you understand the tools on your computer, and your new sales role, e-learning programs are also installed on your laptop. You are given a schedule to complete the learning modules by your supervisor. Whenever you work on an e-learning lesson, your performance is tracked, and a brief progress report is saved to the hard drive of your laptop. Each time you login to your corporate e-mail account, the hard drive is scanned and progress reports are uploaded to a central database. Individuals at headquarters access this information to monitor your training progress. If you are late completing lessons, the system sends you a reminder, as well as a progress report to your supervisor. When you have successfully completed the entire series, it automatically sends you, and your supervisor, a congratulatory message.

LAN Scenario

The organization you work for requires all employees to complete annual training on key topics. They developed a series of training programs just for that purpose. These programs address topics such as workplace safety, customer support, sexual harassment, and the value of diversity. Most of them include video and audio elements. Several even provide options to receive the training in different languages. The training programs reside on CD-ROMs, which can be checked out from the training center and completed at your workstation. As you work through the training, progress reports, indicating the lessons you completed successfully, are automatically reported into your file in the Human Resource Management System (HRMS).

Personal Desktop Assistant (PDA) Scenario

Your job requires you to be on the road for business. However, your trips don't excuse you from the professional development courses you must finish for your next promotion. Your employer determines that, when you travel, you have excess time in hotels, in airports, and on trains that you could use more efficiently. So, to remedy this situation, they provide you with a pocket computer. It is the latest and most advanced version of a Personal Digital Assistant (PDA). The PDA, with its wireless Internet connection, allows you to link into the company's online training programs from almost any location. With this equipment you complete your lessons remotely and have your progress tracked by a Learning Management System (LMS), just as if you were back in the office.

E-LEARNING OR DISTANCE EDUCATION?

Some argue that e-learning and distance education are the same things. However, there is a subtle, but important, difference in the two terms: One puts the emphasis on *learning*; the other puts the emphasis on *education*. Put another way, one helps the learner to grow and develop, while the other is a process for delivering and managing a learning experience. As you describe your efforts, be sure you use the term that accurately communicates your intentions.

HOW LONG WILL E-LEARNING LAST?

How long the term "e-learning" remains in our vocabulary is anyone's guess. But it may be with us for a while. Why? Simply because it is general enough to survive basic advances in technology, yet specific enough to communicate its meaning.

2

Important
e-Learning
Concepts

Each profession contains unique concepts and attributes that define it—e-learning is no exception. Developing your knowledge of those that define e-learning will help you to more fully understand it. I identify and discuss ten such concepts in this chapter. They are presented alphabetically to prevent implying that one is more important than another. In practice, the importance of each is determined by the unique characteristics of a given e-learning project.

Although this chapter might appear as a glossary, these are not simply terms and definitions. To understand e-learning, you must understand the concepts behind and the application of these terms, not just the definitions. Carefully studying each of these explanations before you proceed to subsequent chapters will help you to understand the remainder of this book.

ASSESSMENTS

"Assessments," or tests, help you determine the effectiveness of your e-learning. An assessment challenges the learner to demonstrate a level of understanding and is typically used to document learning outcomes. Well-designed assessments enable the learner to demonstrate mastery of the content presented in the e-learning lessons.

Contrary to what you might expect, the best assessments are developed *before the instruction*. Inexperienced developers sometimes create assessments after the instruction has been designed. The problem with that approach is that the tests measure the effectiveness of lessons, but the lessons may not teach what the learner needs to know. By creating the assessment first, you ensure that it measures what the learner needs to learn. Then, the e-learning is designed to prepare the learner to ace the assessment.

DEVELOPING ASSESSMENTS

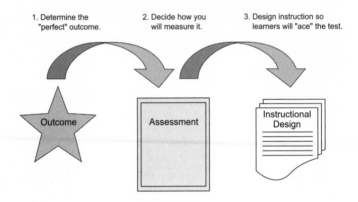

1. Determine the "perfect" outcome.

2. Decide how you will measure it.

3. Design instruction so learners will "ace" the test.

Outcome

Assessment

Instructional Design

DEVELOPING ASSESSMENTS

Assessments test the learning outcomes that lessons, or courses are designed to teach. Therefore, the assessment's style and question type influence the strategies and techniques the designer uses in the lesson's content and practice activities. In the end, by successfully completing an assessment, learners validate the e-learning.

AUTHORING TOOLS

As stated in chapter 1, e-learning relies on computer technology. Not surprisingly, the development of e-learning products requires advanced computer programming. But this "programming" (also called "authoring") is usually not done by computer programmers. Instead, much of the "programming" is done by staff referred to as "developers."

Developers use applications known as "authoring tools" to create e-learning. These are sophisticated software programs designed to simplify production. Many authoring tools consist of pre-programmed routines, which developers populate (fill) with content. Then, the developers sequence the routines to create unique lessons.

Some authoring tools are designed specifically to create e-learning materials. Others are intended for production of such things as Web pages, digital movies or animations. Skilled developers sometimes incorporate lesson components that they develop using different authoring tools into a single lesson. This allows them to take advantage of the various strengths of each tool.

A common misconception—sometimes it's even promoted by the producers of authoring tools!—is that *anyone* can create quality e-learning with a little bit of training. The reality is, most authoring tools take years of on-going use to master. As with the use of any other tool, the person's skill with an authoring tool directly correlates to the quality of the product he or she can produce.

DESIGN DOCUMENTS

Design documents combine the scripts, graphics standard, and production specifications for e-learning products. If you have created traditional training materials, such as self-study guides or videotapes, you will easily grasp the concept of design documents. However, because of the multimedia aspect and complexity of most e-learning projects, e-learning design documents tend to be more elaborate then those of other learning materials.

Just as architectural drawings are the documentation that guides the construction of a building, design documents guide the development of e-learning. An instructional designer develops these documents after a series of analyses are conducted on all relevant aspects of the learning need. These documents communicate volumes: what the developer will program, what graphics the artists make, what audio is recorded by voice talent, which learner interactions are tracked and reported, what reports will be generated, what conditions determine the path a given learner will follow through the lesson, and much more. Design documents streamline and standardize the production of e-learning.

Additionally, design documents are invaluable as archive documentation. Often, after a product is released, you need to modify it. The design document is essential in this instance—it helps you implement a change in the most effective and least intrusive manner.

INSTRUCTIONAL DESIGNERS

Instructional designers offer extensive experience in learning theory, communication theory, psychology and pedagogy. They are specialists in the design and development of learning materials. Many instructional designers specialize in the creation of e-learning. They expanded their knowledge and skills by becoming experts at using technology to deliver interactive learning experiences. Instructional designers with this unique expertise are an essential part of e-learning production teams.

By virtue of their expertise, instructional designers are often asked to assume a leadership role in the production of e-learning materials. They conduct a series of analyses to determine the instructional goals, identify the most effective strategies and techniques for content treatments (such as the use of games, tutorials or simulations), and work with subject matter experts to produce design documents that will guide production.

LEARNING MANAGEMENT SYSTEMS (LMS)

When an organization requires numerous lessons, courses and learners, it may need a Learning Management System (LMS). An LMS provides structure to the learning options, guides the learners to appropriate or mandatory lessons, tracks learner progress and prepares reports.

Most organizations opt to buy or license an LMS, rather than design and build their own. And, many systems are commercially available. I recommend you carefully review and test several systems before you select an LMS for your organization. In addition to the obvious cost issues, you should consider compatibility with existing networks, databases and enterprise-wide systems. Also consider your ability to integrate existing courseware, scalability to meet future needs, and ease of use. See chapter 14 for a complete discussion on LMS.

LEARNING OBJECTS

"Learning objects" are self-contained learning units that meet a clearly defined objective or goal. The theory is, by being kept small and self-contained, learning objects can be mixed, matched and reused to create new lessons. In the late 1990s, as many organizations began to produce substantially more e-learning, interest in learning objects increased dramatically.

The use of learning objects is usually seen as a cost-controlling approach to e-learning development. At first glance, the idea seems sound. But, using learning objects is not a simple thing. Here's an example of what an organization might experience as they consider using learning objects: The Sales Training and Customer Service departments both have identified telephone skills as a training topic. Both groups recognize that all employees must effectively use the telephone to improve their job performance. It seems a single lesson should meet the needs of both departments.

However, upon closer examination, it becomes clear that these are significantly different training situations: the two groups have very different functions within the organization, they deal with different types of phone calls, and the employees have different levels of education, motivation and learning styles.

The learning object concept may fail to adequately train these groups of employees. This leads to the conclusion that using one learning object to train both groups on telephone skills may be a big mistake.

MOTIVATION

For your e-learning to succeed, learners must be motivated to use it. Therefore, understanding what motivates your learners is *essential*. Some learners are motivated by the opportunity to learn. This is called "intrinsic motivation." When self-motivation is high, you can minimize your efforts in designing and implementing motivational strategies.

For other learners, you must generate motivation. This is called "extrinsic motivation." This can be done in any number of ways, such as, creating an engaging game format, recognizing high-scoring individuals, or rewarding everyone that completes the e-learning by a certain date. The most important factor contributing to the success of your e-learning with these learners is the degree to which they value the motivational strategy you put in place.

QUALITY ASSURANCE

Nothing will limit the success of an e-learning activity more than errors in the software. If learners experience errors in software operation, they will lose confidence in the tool and become frustrated by the experience. If learners discover errors in the content or answer judging, they will question the quality and value of the learning experience. Quality assurance (QA) testing is the best way to avoid these problems. QA is the process of finding and fixing errors before the e-learning is released.

The QA process typically involves everyone on the development team, from both the client's and developer's team. Occasionally it involves software testing specialists outside of your organization. See chapter 8 for more information on QA testing.

STANDARDS

A number of efforts have been made to put standards for the design and development of e-learning into widespread use. Some of these initiatives have their roots in industry, while others come from the government.

The Aviation Industry CBT Committee (AICC) developed the most widely known and used standards for e-learning. AICC standards address both Computer-Managed Instruction (CMI) and Computer-Based Training (CBT). Software developed to these standards is referred to as "AICC Certified" or "Designed to AICC Recommendations." While this standard was originally developed for use in the aviation industry, many organizations in other industries are adopting the AICC standards.

The AICC created nine technology-related standards (called "recommendations"). They address areas such as peripheral devices, operating systems, and interfaces.

Two government standards are also worthy of mention:

■ SCORM™—The Sharable Content Object

Reference Model specification consists of a set of technical specifications established by the U.S. Department of Defense. These address issues related to the design, packaging, and delivery of e-learning.

■ Section 508—A second federal government standard, Section 508, refers to a section of the Rehabilitation Act that Congress passed in 1998. This standard speaks to the development of "accessible software," software that can be used by individuals who have limited use of their limbs, are blind, or are deaf. It requires that all government-funded projects be designed to be accessible.

None of these standards is universally applied within the e-learning industry. One of the reasons for this is the rapid rate of technology change. By the time standards are in place the technology has moved to a more advanced stage which is no longer fully addressed by the standard. Another reason is that making products conform to such standards and testing them for compliance can increase the development time and cost of projects.

TYPES OF SOFTWARE

Most e-learning can be placed into one of three categories:

■ Off-the-shelf
■ Template-based
■ Custom-made

Each category has its purpose, and each will fail if used for other than its intended purpose.

"Off-the-self" products are pre-packaged and relatively inexpensive to buy. These are generally developed for mass marketing. Off-the-shelf products tend to address learning needs of predictably large audiences. For example, programs designed to help users learn a new operating system or word processor.

"Template-based" e-learning provides developers with a limited number of software templates, into which they can place content for delivery. These templates tend to be easy to use and highly structured. A developer can use them to create e-learning activities as long as the lessons conform to the pre-designed templates. Using templates can be an effective means of producing instruction for low-level, linear e-learning lessons. However, as the complexity of the content and the learning outcomes increases, the usefulness and appropriateness of the templates decrease.

"Custom-made" e-learning is just what the name implies: e-learning built to meet the specific needs of an organization. The presentation of the content and method of assessment are exactly what works best for the learner and the client. The downsides to this approach are development time and cost. The development of a quality custom lesson takes time and is expensive. There is no doubt that custom-made lessons will be much more costly than either off-the-shelf or template-based lessons. The question is, "Will less expensive approaches meet your e-learning needs?"

3

Who is on the e-Learning Team?

Clients ■

Developers ■

Media Specialists ■

It is important to realize early on: Quality team = Quality product. That is, the quality of an e-learning product directly relates to the expertise of the team producing it. All of your team members should be well-educated and highly experienced in the roles they perform. But, how many members do you need on your learning team? Who should you select? What roles should the team members fill? These are the questions answered in this chapter.

The size of your e-learning team will vary depending on the scope and complexity of your project. For a small project, the team may consist of only a few people who can serve in the roles of production manager, subject matter expert, instructional designer, developer and graphic artist. For more complex projects, or those that are mission critical for your organization, the team can become much larger, involving 15-20 people or more. See the diagram on page 26.

THE e-LEARNING TEAM

Most e-learning teams have three main components, regardless of whether the entire production is done in-house or portions are subcontracted out. Quality e-learning teams contain the following:

■ Client's section

■ Developer's section
■ Media specialist's section

CLIENTS

The client's component of the team consists of the project manager, subject matter expert(s) and reviewers:

■ The product is built for the project manager. He or she manages client resources on the project and coordinates work with the developers. One word of caution: When assembling the client's portion of the team, designate a single person to lead the team and be project manager. More than one person in authorites defuses leadership and slows production. In the end, this may jeopardize the quality of the e-learning.

■ The subject matter expert (SME) is the technical lead for the project. As such, he or she ensures that the most current, accurate and complete information is used while developing the e-learning product.

■ The reviewers check all of the "deliverables" (the individual pieces of documentation and the e-learning product) during the Design and Development stages. They must make sure that the information going into the software is correct. They also verify that the final product is ready for release to the learners.

DEVELOPERS

The developer's component is typically the largest component of the e-learning. It consists of the production manger, instructional designers, developers and graphic artists:

■ The production manager directs and oversees the development of the e-learning. The production manager is also the primary contact with the project manager.

■ The instructional designer conducts the front-end analysis, works with the subject matter experts to identify content, and prepares design documentation for the development team.

■ The graphic artists prepare the visual elements used in the e-learning software. On larger projects, graphic artists may work under the supervision of a creative director. The creative director is responsible for establishing a theme or treatment for the product and ensuring that it is applied consistently throughout development.

■ Developers program the actual e-learning modules and integrate all of the assets into the product. ("Assets" are the individual elements of information used to make e-learning, they are such things as images, text, sound files and animations. Assets are typically produced by the graphic artists and media specialists.)

THE COMPONENTS OF AN e-LEARNING TEAM

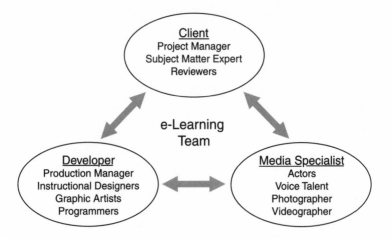

MEDIA SPECIALISTS

Many e-learning development teams also involve a third component consisting of media specialists. As needed, these production experts contribute their talents to create assets.

- Media specialists shoot photos or video, act, provide voices, or serve as studio production crew members for your project. Depending on your specific media needs (which may be restricted by delivery system capabilities) various specialists create assets that the developer integrates into the final product.
- Media requirements differ from project to project, and media production is a limited part

of the development process. Consequently, media specialists are usually subcontractors who have limited roles in the design and development of a product.

4

The Structure of
e-Learning

In chapter 1, I presented several examples of e-learning scenarios. However, e-learning can be much more than a single lesson, or even a course. In this chapter, I discuss the various forms e-learning may take, starting with the largest form, a "university," and working down to the events that make up a lesson.

UNIVERSITIES

An e-learning "university," sometimes referred to as an "online university," should address all the education and training needs of an organization. As you consider e-learning development or begin to assemble an e-learning strategy for your organization, you need to think about the *big picture*. Don't focus on a particular lesson. Instead, consider all of the instruction that your organization uses and needs. From there you can work down to the specific needs of an individual course. This will increase the likelihood that any course you develop will integrate with the long-term strategy of your organization, rather than simply serving a short-term need.

CURRICULAR STRANDS

At a minimum, your university structure should serve all your mission critical needs for employee education and training. This means that a series of coursework needs to be in place to address the learning needs of the various classifications of employees. In addition to the learning experiences needed to meet job requirements, you may choose to incorporate optional personal enrichment or professional development coursework. The goal or desired outcome of each "curricular strand," or sequence of related courses, should be clear and obvious.

In addition to curricular strands that are targeted to meet the needs of employees, many organizations create strands to address the needs of vendors and customers. They see the value in using e-learning strands to attract, train, and retain vendors and customers as part of their competitive strategy.

COURSES

The building blocks of each curricular strand are "courses." More often than not, there is a critical hierarchy to the sequencing of courses. For example, you must learn what your product lines are before you train on their features and competitive advantages.

Course sequences should be structured to ensure they communicate to learners at their level of understanding. Whenever possible, learners should be restricted from taking lessons for which they have not met the entrance requirements. After all, if learners have not completed the prerequisite training, they will struggle to be successful. Their struggles will create a negative impact on their attitude toward learning, and that could reflect badly on the entire e-learning program.

LESSONS

Each course consists of a series of "lessons" or "modules." Each lesson focuses on helping the learner master one or more objectives to achieve the desired learning outcomes. The "mastery of the objectives" within a series of lessons means the learner has reached the education or training goal. The number of lessons needed to achieve a goal depends on the complexity of the course. In fact, a simple course may consist of a single lesson.

The lessons within a course may, or may not, have a learning hierarchy associated with them. When no hierarchy exists, let learners choose a path through the lessons. However, if a hierarchy does exist, cluster lessons that are at the same level of prerequisite knowledge and allow learners to choose their learning path through each cluster.

Events of Instruction

By now you may have noticed a pattern: Each subsequent level I have described is a building block for the previously described level. The Events of Instruction, a learning model proposed by Robert Gagné, are no exception. Gagné identified nine distinct events of instruction (see table on page 34). In my work, I have repeatedly found that each fulfills a specific function in the learning process. When all nine events are present in a lesson, the learning opportunity is "optimal." The more events that are left out during the development of a lesson, the greater the likelihood the lesson will fail.

I tend to cluster the nine Events of Learning into three broad categories:

- **Pre-Instructional**—These activities focus the learners' attention on the lesson and prepare them to learn.

- **Instructional**—These activities present new content and help the learners retain it.
- **Post-Instructional**—These activities demonstrate learning occurred. They provide an opportunity for the learners to reinforce what they learned by applying it.

Organizing lessons this way helps me understand the sequencing of events and the role they play in the design and development of successful instruction.

The table below briefly elaborates and categorizes the Events of Instruction described above. A wide array of strategies and techniques are available to use in each event. The treatment of each event is limited only by the creativity of the designer and the capabilities of the e-learning delivery system.

LESSON STRUCTURE

	Pre-Instruction	Instruction	Post-Instruction
Events of Instruction	• Gain the learners' attention. • Tell the learners what they will be expected to learn. • Help the learners to understand how this relates to other learning.	• Present content. • Provide strategies or techniques to help the learners retain and retrieve the content. • Involve the learners in practice activities • Give the learners feedback.	• Assess the learners' understanding of the lesson content. • Provide strategies or techniques to help the learners transfer their learning and apply it in activities outside the lesson.

Adapted from Gagné, R. M., Briggs, L. J. and Wager, W. W. (1992). *Principles of Instructional Design*, (4th ed.). New York: Holt, Rinehart and Winston, table 10-1.

Section Two

This section consists of eight chapters. They focus on the complete lifecycle of an e-learning product. The lifecycle model described is one I created. Over the past decade, I developed and refined the model to assist me in communicating with our e-learning development partners. This section is intended to alert developers to what they should expect during production and how they can most constructively support an e-learning product or initiative.

5

Introduction to the
Lifecycle Model

LIFECYCLE OF AN E-LEARNING PRODUCT

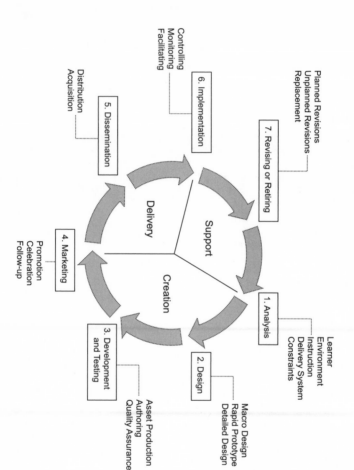

E-learning costs money—and nobody likes to see money wasted. So, with rare exception, e-learning products are developed for long-term use. However, based upon my observations, organizations that fund e-learning development seldom have a clear idea of what a product's expected life span will be. Further, they are even less likely to understand the stages of its lifecycle and how their efforts at various stages can extend the life span of an e-learning program.

The lifecycle of an e-learning product is comprised of three general phases, and seven stages that involve specific tasks. Each stage represents an essential part of the product's natural evolution. Just as neglecting to address all nine Events of Instruction (chapter 4) may result is a less effective lesson, neglecting to address any of these seven stages could negatively impact the success of your e-learning.

Creation

This is the first phase. It consists of Analysis, Design, and Development. The creation phase has one primary goal: the creation of the most effective and useful product for the given situation.

Delivery

This is the second phase. It consists of Marketing and Dissemination. The delivery phase has two primary goals: to get the intended audience interested in the e-learning product and to get the product distributed to the learners.

Support

This is the final phase. It consists of Implementation and Revision/Retirement. The support phase has one goal: to keep the e-learning product in use, and optimally effective, for as long as possible.

The remaining chapters in this section discuss the various stages in the lifecycle. These chapters will help you to understand how each of these goals listed above is met.

6

Analysis

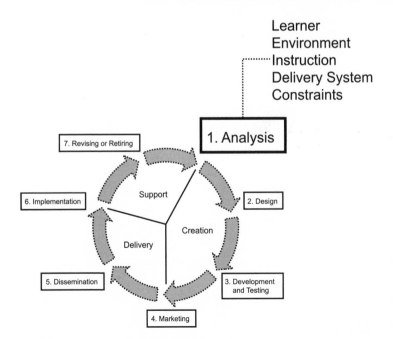

Learner
Environment
Instruction
Delivery System
Constraints

1. Analysis

7. Revising or Retiring

6. Implementation

Support

5. Dissemination

Delivery

Creation

2. Design

3. Development
and Testing

4. Marketing

L et's review a basic point: Training is developed to address a *need*. When new employees are joining your organization, you need to train them. When a new product is released, you need to tell people about it. When new procedures are implemented, your employees need to learn them. Unfortunately, not all of your organization's problems are solved with training. Other issues, such as the volume of work, quality of raw materials, age of equipment or labor concerns, can create problems that training cannot solve.

When a problem is identified in your organization, someone within your organization must conduct a needs assessment to determine whether the problem can be solved through training. If you determine that training is a viable option, an instructional designer should conduct some additional investigations. Collectively, this series of analyses is called a "front-end analysis."

The purpose of a front-end analysis is to determine the most effective method for addressing the learning need. Until these analyses are completed, it is impossible to know what the best solution will be. Unfortunately, clients (the people for whom the training is developed) often have a training concept in mind long before the front-end analysis begins. The clients may want a computer-based simulation that can also be used as a sales tool. Or, perhaps they may want an Internet-delivered lesson, which employees can access from offices around the world. Whatever their desire, in these cases the instructional designer is forced to try to design the best solution possible given the delivery method this client is imposing—usually not the most effective approach.

The front-end analysis stage examines the following five areas:

- Learner characteristics
- Scope and nature of the content
- Learning environment
- Delivery system
- Project constraint

When implemented properly, your front-end analysis will guide you to the most appropriate method for delivering your training. Furthermore, it will establish a number of parameters that will guide the production process. Findings of the front-end analysis are captured in a high-level description of your proposed solution. This document, known as a "Macro Design Document," is used to obtain consensus among stakeholders before the more costly design and development tasks are undertaken. The five areas examined during a front-end analysis are described below.

LEARNER ANALYSIS

Knowledge of your training audience (the learners for your product) can dramatically affect your e-learning design.

During this analysis, explore learner characteristics that impact how users approach and interact with the instruction. Some of the questions you need to answer are:

- How similar or different are the learners?
- What are their ages, genders, skills and aptitudes?
- Do they have prior knowledge or experience that will influence how they approach this learning experience?
- What will motivate them to participate and to do well in the training?

The information you gain by asking such questions influences the decisions you make later in the design process. For example, you may discover that your intended audience represents several different groups of learners, such as office staff, field staff, managers and IT specialists. While some of the information they need to learn is common across all groups, there is also information unique to each group. Your training design will need to address this issue in a way that keeps the learners focused and engaged. Or, you may find that your learners are diverse in other ways, such as language and culture. This may influence you to provide the instruction in multiple languages that are localized to the learners' cultures.

INSTRUCTIONAL ANALYSIS

Knowledge about the content, requirements for content presentation, practice activities, learner feedback, and learner assessment all influence how you design the training software. This is called "instructional analysis". In this analysis mode, the instructional designer determines answers to critical questions, such as:

- At what level should the instruction begin?
- What learning outcomes are needed—facts, concepts, rules or procedures?
- Is there a hierarchical order to the information you need to cover?
- What must the learner do to demonstrate that he or she has learned?

As a result of the instructional analysis, you may opt to "chunk" (that is, cluster) information together into segments based on a content hierarchy. Or, you may decide to blend both online and offline activities. Your options are nearly infinite.

ENVIRONMENTAL ANALYSIS

This area of analysis, called "environmental analysis," is usually a brief, but sometimes critical, component of the discovery process. Knowing the conditions under which your e-learning solutions will be used can radically influence how you design the e-learning. You must consider a number of questions related to the learning environment:

- Is the learning environment clean and dry?
- Is it quiet?
- Is there the potential for frequent interruptions?
- Are there sufficient electrical outlets for the e-learning equipment?
- What level of security is available to protect equipment?

After answering these questions, you may recommend that all training workstations come with headphones. Or, maybe you'll suggest that all keyboards be covered with plastic membranes to keep them clean. You might recognize that all your e-learning lessons must be brief and allow for interruptions. Or, maybe you'll add a bookmark feature for learners to mark their place in the lesson and return to it later. Of course, depending on what you find in your analysis, you will need to adjust your design to accommodate for it.

DELIVERY SYSTEM ANALYSIS

This area of analysis, called "delivery system analysis," involves examining the entire training system you will use to deliver and support your e-learning. You will need to consider computer capabilities, network connections, the nature of the database where records will be stored, the availability of mentors for the learners, existing resources or potential job aids and many other issues. By asking questions that relate to the entire system, you can determine how to best design and integrate e-learning into the curriculum.

Findings from your delivery system analysis directly affect the design and delivery of your e-learning training modules. For example, if database storage space is at a premium, you may determine that only each learner's completion data will be tracked and stored. If some computers do not have sound cards, audio narration will not be an option for your training. Or, if there is a high ratio of supervisors to trainees, structured mentoring activities may be included in the design to allow learners to apply what they are learning in a carefully supervised situation.

CONSTRAINT ANALYSIS

This area of analysis, called "constraint analysis," explores the resource limitations that will determine the parameters for development of your e-learning. Constraints examined during this analysis fall into three categories:

- Timetable
- Human resources
- Capital resources

When conducting this type of analysis, you should ask these questions:

- What is the budget for the project?
- When must the training be available for use?
- Does all of the training have to be released at the same time?
- How many people will be signing-off at project milestones? Who are they?
- What is the availability of subject matter experts (SMEs) to review the design documents?
- Are the SMEs' reviews part of their normal workload, or has this been added to otherwise full sets of responsibilities?
- What percentage of SMEs' time will be committed to the project?

As you can see, some of these questions may be difficult for the client to answer, but the answers are critical to the success of the project. For example, if there is a group of individuals who are responsible for giving approval (signing-off) at project milestones, sign-offs will take you longer to obtain. Also, working with multiple signers may require more revisions, so that everyone's concerns are addressed, before approval can be obtained. Or, if the timetable is short or the budget is low, you may need to keep the production value of the e-learning to a minimum.

At the conclusion of the front-end analysis stage, the instructional designer should prepare a Macro Design Document. The purpose of this document is to present the findings, discuss their impact on the overall design and communicate a plan to proceed with the project. Based on what is communicated, the training client may want to discuss alternatives. These might include extending the timetable, increasing the budget or allocating additional staff. Additionally, it is each stakeholder's responsibility to challenge any findings that are inconsistent with his or her understanding of the learning needs or proposed project. The Macro Design Document should spur discussion and lead to a common understanding of the e-learning project among all concerned.

7

Design

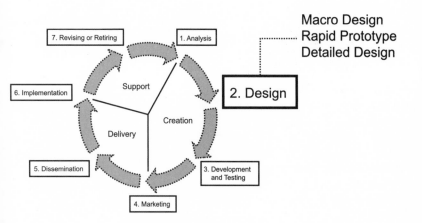

7. Revising or Retiring

1. Analysis

Support

2. Design

Macro Design
Rapid Prototype
Detailed Design

6. Implementation

Creation

Delivery

3. Development
and Testing

5. Dissemination

4. Marketing

The Macro Design Document, completed by the instructional designer, reports the findings of the front-end analysis. It provides a high-level view of the e-learning project. In it, the instructional designer addresses many broad issues, such as who the learners are, the scope of the content, general instructional teatment, basic motivational strategies, the development timetable and budget. However, this document also focuses on the findings of the analysis and the general direction these findings indicate the training should take. It is not intended to provide the specificity needed to enable the team to proceed to the development stage.

A Detailed Design Document is necessary before e-learning development can begin. The project's lead instructional designer writes the Detailed Design Document while working with key members of the production team, including the creative director and lead programmer. This document must capture the smallest details of the project and communicate how they interrelate with the specificity required to guide production of the e-learning software.

There are numerous issues that the Detailed Design Document must communicate to the development team.

For example, pages describing the instructional presentation must address the following:

- **Information Treatments**–Presenting content and directions, including sequencing the presentation of instructional text, graphics, narration, informational audio and video.
- **Orientation Strategies**–Communicating to learners their location within the software. Strategies include the use of headers, subheaders, icons, colors and page numbers.
- **Navigation Techniques**–Establishing functions that allow learners to move from place to place in the software, including menus, buttons and links.
- **Aesthetics Elements**–Representing appropriate culture, mood, status and attitude, through the use of colors, images, sounds and font styles.
- **Featured Tools**–Providing support devices, including such things as bookmarks, notepads and calculators.

Of course, there are many aspects of an e-learning application that are not as obvious to learners as the instructional presentation. These must also be clearly documented in the Detailed Design Document. They include the following:

- **Adaptive Designs**–Strategies to modify the presentation of the instruction to better accommodate the unique characteristics of a learner or category of learners.

- **Learner Management**–Strategies for directing learners to the appropriate areas of study based on job requirements or patterns of performance.
- **Record Keeping/Security**–Techniques for tracking time on tasks, items presented, responses, scores, options selected, progress, etc., and limiting access to this information based on established criteria.
- **Reporting**–Methods for customizing and filing individual and/or group reports (electronically or in print) to the learner, as well as the organization.
- **Administration**–Features for adding or deleting students and for modifying instructional requirements, such as mastery criteria.

All of the information in the Detailed Design Document must be consistent with the Macro Design Document. When this is not possible, perhaps due to a shift in the scope or direction of the project, an explanation with supporting justification must be provided to the stakeholders. In addition, the content must be consistent with current theories and practices in message design, instructional design, adult learning, motivation and assessment.

A written instructional design serves several other purposes in addition to its primary role of guiding development. These include the following:

- It allows the developers and clients to "desk check" (or verify) the logic and flow of the design before production begins.

■ It provides an easy means for the SME to review the content and make edits prior to production, thereby controlling cost.

■ It serves as a "blueprint," which can be archived for reference if modification becomes necessary in the future.

Creation of a sound Detailed Design Document is an essential component of an e-learning product's lifecycle. Failure to do an adequate job at this point in the process will almost certainly result in cost overruns, missed or inappropriately covered content, and ineffective training.

8

Development and
Testing

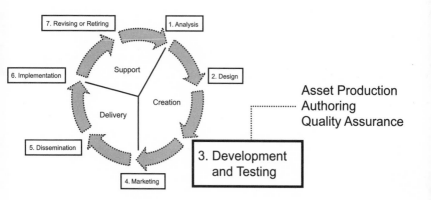

Asset Production
Authoring
Quality Assurance

All of the preceding analysis and design work takes shape now, during the Development Stage. This is when your team actually *creates* the e-learning product. The Development Stage is extremely intense and demanding for team members on both the development and client side.

Using the Detailed Design Document as a guide, your development team produces or secures all of the media assets (such as graphics, photographs, animations, narrations, sound effects and video). Then, the developer uses the authoring tool to assemble and present the assets. Of course, the authoring must also incorporate all the required navigation, orientation, interaction, management, record keeping and administrative features. All this is thoroughly specified in the Detailed Design Document.

Prior to development, people new to e-learning seldom value the amount of analysis and design work that is undertaken during a project. However, once development begins, it is all justified—and appreciated. The effort put forth in determining learner motivation, preferences for graphic styles, prior experience with e-learning, and countless other details, begins to pay off now. Why? Because the development team has the information they need to create an e-learning product they know will be effective.

All of the tough decisions are made during the analysis and design stages. Once it has been reviewed and approved by the SMEs, the Detailed Design Document (DDD) becomes a "recipe book" that the production team will follow. For example, using the specified naming convention provided in the documentation by the instructional designer, the graphic artist labels and stores newly created images. In turn, the developer referring to the documentation quickly identifies the correct graphic file he or she needs for a particular module. Then, following the documentation, he or she can integrate the asset at the correct location in the program being authored.

Because everyone is following the same directions (the DDD) this work is accomplished with a minimum effort and a high degree of confidence. The DDD expedites production by being a common source with *all* the details needed by the production team. These details range from the sequencing of presentation elements to performance tracking requirements, audio scripts and the file formats needed to export data.

AUTHORING

Authoring is the use of development tools to create e-learning products. There are many different development tools on the market. In fact, as a result of the industry practice of "upgrading" software products, there are many versions of some tools currently in use. Third party add-ons are available for many development tools. These add-ons extend the capability of the development tool.

Each development tool on the market has a special niche. Some emphasize their ability to deliver large volumes of graphics, animations and audio. Others specialize in interactive presentations, answer judging and tracking performance. Selection of specific development tools should be guided by a few basic questions:

- How will your instruction be delivered? Over a low bandwidth connection to a PDA, from a CD-ROM on the user's workstation, or some other method?
- What are the dominant characteristics of your lesson design? Does it require lots of animation, video and audio? Does it contain high levels of interactivity and require tracking larger volumes of learner statistics?
- Who will be responsible for authoring and maintaining the e-learning and what programs have they worked with? What is their skill level?
- What other systems must the e-learning "communicate" with inside your organization?

Both development tools and developers have their limitations. When your team is designing a lesson, you need to keep these limitations in mind. Otherwise, your vision may exceed your reach.

QUALITY ASSURANCE TESTING

In addition to implementing the design, all team members must be involved in several levels of quality assurance testing (the process of eliminating errors in the e-learning product). Quality assurance (QA) tests are conducted throughout the development stage. QA is an on-going process, and it is *absolutely critical to your release of a high-quality product*. QA has one fundamental goal: ensure the e-learning is free of both operational and content errors, including omissions.

Note that QA testing and "formative evaluation" (see chapter 13) share some common objectives and may be conducted simultaneously. However, these are very different activities, with different goals, and shouldn't be confused.

Several different rounds of QA testing are conducted throughout the development process. Each round takes advantage of the strengths of the various members of the development team. The different rounds of QA, the team members involved, and the purpose of that round are described below.

QA Round 1–The Developers

Developers are responsible for conducting the first round of QA testing. It is their job to test the software, to ensure that it is fully functional and error-free before a module is made available for review by others. The developer must test *all* of the functions within each module. Errors identified during this round of testing are fixed immediately by the developer.

Even the most thorough developer testing the software will not discover all the errors in the module. Sometimes this happens because he or she is "too close" to the project and fails to see an error because he or she has been looking at it too long. Other times, he or she is too familiar with how the software should operate and does not test "non-standard" ways of using it. Or, the developer's testing workstation might not accurately reflect the environment in which the learner will use the tool. The workstation may not provide a true test of how the program will operate on the target platform. So, your team must perform additional tests to eliminate potential problems.

QA Round 2–The Instructional Designers

Once the developers complete their testing, the instructional designers begin their review of the software. While they will continue to look for operational errors, the primary goal of this round of testing is to verify completeness and accuracy. To accomplish this, the instructional designers compare the e-learning program to the Detailed Design Document. Any errors they identify are entered into an error-tracking log. That log is maintained throughout the QA process to monitor and manage both the reporting and resolution of errors.

QA Round 3–The Client Team

When the development team believes all functional and content errors are found and resolved, the client team should now take a look. The focus of their review is to make sure that the content is accurately presented, that the assets support the content as intended, and the assessments are working as needed. Although the SMEs reviewed the Detail Design Document, they don't see the actual presentation of the content until the software is operational.

When working with highly technical content, it is not uncommon, for example, for the SMEs to find that an image is out of place. In the case of something like an x-ray, it may even be upside down.

The client team must focus on four things while reviewing the content:

- Content errors
- Omissions
- Sequencing problems related to the content treatment and presentation
- Operational errors that were missed in the previous QA testing

Any errors they discover should be reported into the error-tracking log.

Your e-learning team may need to complete their testing several times as errors are discovered, resolved, and the fixes are validated. Following this, your team should be confident that the product is tested internally to the fullest extent possible.

QA Round 4 A–Outside Testing (optional)

After your team has exhaustively tested the product, you may want to employ an outside testing group to verify that the product is error-free. Whether or not to use an outside testing group depends on the following:

- The nature of the e-learning content
- Scope of the project
- Liabilities associated with a potential error in the training
- Your budget
- The project timetable

One potential advantage of using an outside company specializing in software testing is they can test your product on many hardware and network configurations. Another advantage is that you have a completely fresh set of eyes looking at the software.

The risks with this approach are the costs, time spent in testing, and exposure of what may be proprietary information to an outside group. Furthermore, you may receive a long list of suggested format changes that may not really represent bugs, but still require your team's attention to review and discuss.

QA Round 4 B–Field Testing (optional, but recommended)

Another QA option is to conduct a limited field trial on a controlled basis with learners that represent your intended audience. This option is sometimes known as "beta testing." This approach has the advantage of using the e-learning product on the actual delivery system and with a real group of learners.

The greatest risk with a field test is that, if it goes badly, it could affect the success of the product implementation. If the e-learning product doesn't operate properly during testing, learners might become frustrated and disappointed by the experience. Their negative attitude toward the e-learning could be spread throughout the organization before the product is officially released. So, be sure the e-learning is ready to be used before you involve employees outside of your development team.

9

Marketing

- 7. Revising or Retiring
- 1. Analysis
- 6. Implementation
- 2. Design
- Support
- Creation
- Delivery
- 5. Dissemination
- 3. Development and Testing

4. Marketing

Promotion
Celebration
Follow-up

Q: What one word best describes the Marketing Stage of e-learning?

A: Overlooked.

It is not surprising that a core team consisting largely of trainers and developers focuses primarily on aspects of design, development and delivery. However, if you want your product to be used, you need to let people know about it and build their expectations about what it will do for them. The benefits gained from marketing your product are well worth the effort. So, announce the product to management and captivate your learners' attention. It will dramatically increase product use.

Marketing is just as important for internal products as for those intended for use with customers or vendors. The idea behind e-learning marketing is simple. It should increase use by accomplishing six things:

1. Make people aware of the product while it is under development.
2. Let them know who will use it.
3. Explain how it will benefit them and their organization.
4. Communicate the release date.

5. Celebrate the implementation of the training.
6. Follow-up with periodic announcements and reports.

Your pre-release marketing activities prepare learners for the e-learning. These activities raise learner awareness, establish expectations about how learners will benefit, foster anticipation, and increase their perceived value of the e-learning program.

Having a launch ceremony or celebration when the e-learning program is released can be a powerful marketing tool. It is an effective way to recognize the contributions of those who worked hard to make the e-learning a reality. Also, it emphasizes the importance of the program—and motivates learners to participate in using it.

Follow-up, or post-release, marketing keeps the momentum going and extends the life of the e-learning. An article in a newsletter reporting the launch of the e-learning, periodic e-mail messages updating the status of the completion rate, or posted reminders encouraging compliance with the training can all reinforce the importance placed on the product by your organization. Each communication can heighten learners' awareness of the program and encourage participation.

In total, these marketing activities elevate the e-learning experience from that of an isolated set of training events to an integral part of your work environment. When you invest even the minimum in marketing, you can reap significant benefits. This effort drastically enhances the perception of, and participation in, your e-learning initiative.

You can use these common forms of internal marketing to build interest in and anticipation for your e-learning:

- Publish articles in newsletters that are distributed to learners.
- Place posters around the office that announce the e-learning project.
- Display information about the e-learning project in common areas.
- Send out e-mail announcements that broadcast the training opportunity.
- Develop special Web pages that serve as teasers. They can provide progress reports and sample lessons for the training.
- Conduct an official "ribbon cutting" ceremony or open house and invite prominent individuals as your guests of honor.

It's also important to recognize that sometimes *no amount of marketing* generates the interest and learning commitment that your organization needs. In these situations, you may have to simultaneously implement an incentive program that encourages participation. These programs typically offer inducements for learners to invest themselves in the e-learning experience. Depending on the structure of the program, each individual may be directly compensated. Or, learners may compete for a limited number of awards based on their completion times or test scores. Be creative. You might be surprised at how effective your ideas are.

Reward and recognition programs are most appropriate in the following instances:

- When the timetable for completing the learning is very short.
- When the volume of content the learners must complete is exceptionally large.
- When learners are otherwise poorly motivated to engage in the training.

Such programs need to be carefully structured to ensure the maximum impact is achieved. Companies that sell incentive items are often able to help design and manage incentive programs that support your training program. Obviously, such programs require additional cost. However, when conditions warrant, it can be well worth the investment.

You need to market your e-learning, regardless of whether it's for a relatively small, local group of learners, or for every employee in a global corporation. Your e-learning will thrive because of it. Marketing should never be overlooked.

10

Dissemination

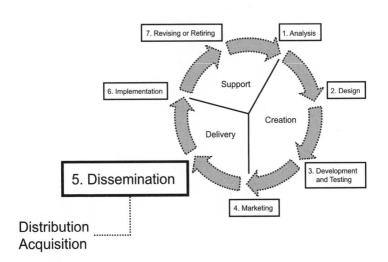

- 7. Revising or Retiring
- 1. Analysis
- 2. Design
- 6. Implementation
- Support
- Creation
- Delivery
- 3. Development and Testing
- 5. Dissemination
- 4. Marketing

Distribution
Acquisition

Once your e-learning product is finished, perhaps even while you are marketing it, the Dissemination Stage begins. This stage consists of two components: Distribution and Acquisition. Both components are essential to the successful rollout of your product. The first is typically given adequate consideration. The second is often ignored.

DISTRIBUTION

"Distribution," making the software available to those who will use it, is usually the most obvious and easily accomplished task in the lifecycle. The groundwork for distributing your e-learning product begins early in the Analysis Stage. At that point, you determine the location of your audience, you study the learning environment, you analyze the delivery system, and you plan out how the software will be made available. This groundwork makes distribution a simple process.

Whether you distribute the software via Internet, intranet, extranet, CD-ROM or DVD-ROM, there are two basic strategies you must consider. These are commonly referred to as "push" and "pull."

The Push Strategy

The Push Strategy, where the e-learning is "pushed out" to the learner, is the most common. The software, assuming it is tangible, is mailed to the learner or the learner's supervisor. From there, the learner is directed to complete the training. Or, if you created an online product, such as Web-based training, the learner may simply receive an e-mail with a link to the login and instructions to complete the training by a given date. In both cases, the learner receives the product from you directly. This strategy works best when your learners are externally motivated, are required to complete training, and when someone will closely monitor to see that the learners complete the training.

The Pull Strategy

The Pull Strategy is less direct. It relies on learners to access learning modules on their own. In this strategy, your courses might be available online. Or, maybe you have the software in learning centers at your various corporate offices. Regardless of where the training resides, it is up to the learner to seek out and complete the training. To attain high levels of participation, you may want to motivate learners to take part in the training initiative. For example, your organization may establish a policy of promoting only those individuals who have completed a series of courses. Or, you may put into place a program in which employees who complete training modules earn recognition points they can spend on prizes.

The Pull Strategy is most effective when learners are highly self-motivated. When this is the situation, learners

76

just need to know that the learning is available. An incentive program is unnecessary.

ACQUISITION

"Acquisition," getting buy-in and acceptance from those who will supervise or use the software, can be difficult to obtain. This is partially because acquisition activities are seldom seen as part of a product's lifecycle. But they are an important stage that should not be treated lightly because of the risk of seriously underutilizing the e-learning. If that happens, the potential value derived from e-learning suffers. Many organizations mistakenly think, "If we develop e-learning, employees will use it." What if the more likely outcome occurs? No one accesses the training. The benefits you hope to realize from the investment are never attained.

To be successful in promoting acquisition, you need to understand a little bit of psychology. Remember, most employees' primary concern is for their jobs. Their jobs are demanding and time-consuming, and the employees are highly accountable for seeing that their job is done well. Some, at least in the short term, feel that training will keep them from getting their work done. Consequently, many employees see training as something extra that you are adding to their workload. These employees often have difficulty justifying the investment of time and effort for the training. To further complicate the situation, supervisors are under pressure to "get the work done with the resources available." All too often, these supervisors don't see the value of promoting training if it takes employees away from "their work." Both employee and supervisor need to believe in the value of the training.

So, you need to apply some psychology of your own. Be sure you communicate the value of training to everyone in the organization. The learners within your organization need to hear from management that being well-trained is part of each employee's "work." Then employees need to know that you are developing training specifically for them. Give them the specifics. If you're developing compliance training, explain the corporate need for the training. Also explain the corporate risks if they fail to comply. If you're developing job skill training, make sure the supervisors see how training fits into short-term and long-term strategies. Help them understand the benefits they will derive from the training.

This process should begin in the Marketing Stage (chapter 9) and often helps to improve both supervisor and employee motivation levels. It's also important for you to continue your acquisition efforts well into the Dissemination Stage. After helping the supervisors and employees see the big picture, you need to keep up your efforts so the thought stays in their minds. Regardless of whether your e-learning product is pushed or pulled to the learners, if you can maintain a high level of buy-in, your product is destined to succeed.

11

Implementation

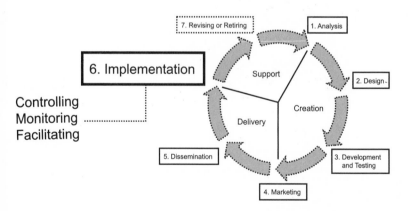

As you complete the Dissemination Stage, learners begin to use your software. At this point in the life-cycle, the Implementation Stage begins. This stage involves controlling and monitoring, while you continue to promote your product's use. These activities are intended to ensure that your organization benefits from all the learning outcomes you planned.

Depending on the nature of your e-learning, you may choose to have a select group of learners use it. Or, you may make it available to everyone in your organization. If your network or Internet capacity is limited, you have a number of ways to restrict who can use the software. For example, in smaller implementations you can pre-register learners and compare the login entries against a list of approved users. This can be accomplished by building an administrative feature into the software. By using this feature, an instructor or supervisor can enter a list of approved training participants into your Learning Management System (LMS). In large scale implementations, you may want to announce the availability of the e-learning on a regional or country basis. This can occur over a period of days or weeks to prevent overloading your system.

Usually, e-learning implementations are on a timetable. You may need to meet a government-mandated compliance requirement by a specific date. Or, maybe you need to train your employees on your upcoming year's product line before it hits the street. Regardless of what is driving your implementation timetable, you will have to monitor learner access to and use of the e-learning software. This activity is called "implementation monitoring."

Although you can automate some aspects of implementation monitoring, typically it is your training manager's responsibility to enforce the training timetable. For example, using an LMS-generated report of learners who are not completing the training on schedule, the training manager must determine the appropriate course of action. Should learners be contacted? What should they be told? The software alone cannot make these decisions or act upon them.

Another significant role for the training manager is that of "promoter." Based on the performance requirements and the timetable allowed for training, a training manager should contact the learners and provide support, encouragement and advice to them. Some learners assume, when the entire training experience is restricted to the computer, that no one is tracking their training efforts. As a result, learners allow themselves to get distracted by other obligations. A well-timed e-mail encouraging learners to continue working on a lesson may be just what they need to motivate them to finish. Training managers must develop their skills with the tools they need for monitoring learning and communicating with learners.

Finally, the reusability of e-learning means that implementation will be repeated many times. As such, the implementation process for your organization must be on-going until the software is no longer in use. It's not uncommon, over the life of a product, to gather huge volumes of user records. You must decide what to do with all of the data. Questions to consider include the following:

■ What information in the learners' records will you keep?
■ How long will you keep the records?
■ Who has the authority to delete old records?

Careful attention to these matters throughout the Implementation Stage ensures that your e-learning product is used to the fullest extent possible. As a result, you reap the fullest possible benefits from your e-learning: Your learners achieve success, and your organization obtains statistics documenting learner participation.

12

Revising or Retiring

Planned Revisions
Unplanned Revisions
Replacement

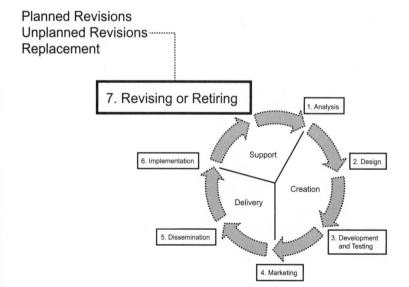

7. Revising or Retiring

1. Analysis

2. Design

3. Development and Testing

4. Marketing

5. Dissemination

6. Implementation

Support

Creation

Delivery

Congratulations! Your e-learning program is up and running. You see your organization improving as a direct result of your extensive efforts. Now what?

After all your work getting an e-learning program rolled out, you probably don't want to think about the next phase in the e-learning lifecycle: Revising or Retiring. But you should. Part of any training effort—and e-learning is no exception—is planning to maintain and eventually to discontinue using a product.

At a minimum, the scope and complexity of most e-learning programs virtually guarantee that your development team will need to make changes after the initial release. Some of these changes may be planned. You may know right from the outset that the e-learning will eventually need to be translated and offered in several languages. Other changes may be unanticipated. For example, shortly after the e-learning version of your new employee orientation is completed, your company adds a new line of products that you haven't covered.

When the need to make changes occurs, who makes the changes, and the ease with which the changes are made, will directly relate to how well you planned for this eventuality. Planning should have occurred during Design and Development stages.

PLANNED REVISIONS

It's common to realize, at the very beginning of e-learning development projects, that someone must modify the final software after it is released. Maybe you're anticipating scalability: You plan to add modules over time. This, of course, requires scalable menus and record-keeping features. Maybe you realize that the training content is time-sensitive: The pricing on your products requires updating as your costs change. Whatever specifics lead to your planned changes, the key is *early identification* and *clear articulation* of the need. When this is done, you can build into your plan how you will make the changes. One way is to choose certain tools for developing the e-learning that you are already familiar with. Another is to automate the updates by linking them to another application. Or, you may decide to use file structures that are external to the e-learning application and are easy to edit. Without a doubt, you will need to identify the specific update process before the product is authored, if you want to easily implement revisions.

When you know you will be responsible for post-release revisions, you need to establish a knowledge transfer process with your development team. Knowledge transfer involves having developers train your training staff to maintain the e-learning and to implement minor revisions. The process will build in-house expertise and reduce reliance on external vendors.

What difference does it make which development tools you use? Well, your choice of development tools influences who is capable of completing post-release revisions. If you want to rely upon in-house staff to make the changes, your development tools must be limited, basic and easy to use. And your staff must already be familiar with these tools, or they must have the aptitude to learn them with minimal effort.

Why worry about the file structure you use when developing your e-learning? The answer is simple; some file structures make revisions easy for an entry level developer to implement, and others require an expert. For example, if you plan to replace graphics or photographs, where the images reside is an important consideration. When you anticipate that these assets will change, keep them in external libraries, rather than packaged with the code. This simple decision at the beginning of development makes their replacement much easier and less expensive for you.

At the start of a project, think through the need for updates and revisions. If you can clearly identify specific changes that will be on-going or recurring, you may want to consider building a tool to automate the revision process. Such a tool might allow basic computer users to import audio, graphics and text that can automatically replace outdated information.

UNPLANNED REVISIONS

Over a period of time many things can change. Some of these changes will require you to revise your e-learning program:

■ Companies merge or are acquired.

- Names are changed.
- People leave the organization.
- Procedures are updated.
- Products are replaced.
- Uniforms get a new look.

Perhaps the impact of one change may not significantly reduce the effectiveness of your software. But as more of these inconsistencies and inaccuracies creep into the software, they affect the perceived quality and value of the program. If your organization continues to use the e-learning, someone must revise it.

SOURCE CODE CHANGES

Many programs can only be revised if you have access to the source code. Source code is the programming code as it exists prior to packaging for final release. Once code has been packaged, it cannot be edited. Therefore, when contracting with an outside provider, it is *absolutely critical* that your agreement *states that you own the source code*. You also need to see that the code is archived for later use if needed. In addition, your contract should state that the source code must be carefully documented so that a programmer who had not worked on it originally could understand and modify it. Finally, it is important that your contract states *no proprietary tools* are used in the development of your e-learning. If you do not absolutely ensure these things are resolved prior to development, you may not be able to make the changes you need.

Just because your in-house staff has access to the source code, doesn't mean that they *should make* the revisions. Any revisions, other than simple graphic or text changes, can have a ripple effect on your e-learning product. This could dramatically alter how your software operates. In the worst case, it could render it inoperable.

Consult the Detailed Design Document before anyone considers altering the code. If the revision is too complex or risky, you may opt to outsource the revisions you need.

REPLACEMENT

Just as most e-learning programs will need some revisions over time, there also comes a time when a program is no longer applicable. Any number of circumstances could bring about the replacement of your e-learning program:

- The changes it needs are too extensive and require too great a cost.
- Your pool of learners is so different now that they require significantly different training.
- The training need no longer exists.

Regardless of the reason, it is important to accept that the life of every e-learning product ends. There are two main ways that an e-learning program ends:

- It is eliminated outright.
- It is replaced.

Your decision on how to proceed should be based on the results of a new Needs Assessment. This activity brings you full circle—back to the beginning of the e-Learning Product Lifecycle.

Section Three

This final section consists of three chapters. Through them I present information on large-scale and overarching issues that relate to e-learning. Specifically, these chapters discuss the four modes of evaluation you need to conduct throughout the life of a product, the content management system attributes and applications, and how you can determine the value of an e-learning product.

13

Evaluation

A s you have seen in the previous chapters, delivery of a quality e-learning product takes considerable planning and effort. And, to be sure that your efforts are directed in the most appropriate ways, you need continuous evaluations.

There are four types of evaluation that need to be implemented:

- Formative evaluation, which is conducted to ensure the elements that make up your product are accurate and effective with the intended learners; this evaluation spans the Design and Development and Testing Stages.

- Summative evaluation, which is conducted to determine the effectiveness and efficiency of the e-learning; this spans the Development and Testing, Marketing, and Dissemination Stages.

- Maintenance evaluation, which is conducted to identify modifications that may be required to the software; this spans from the Implementation Stage through the Revising or Retiring Stage.

- Process evaluation, which is conducted to identify process improvements; this spans the entire lifecycle.

Together, these four types of evaluation encompass the entire lifecycle of a project. The first three combine to determine a product's appeal, accuracy, functionality, thoroughness and effectiveness. These evaluations are conducted so that the best possible learning product is produced. The final form of evaluation is used to evaluate the process your team uses in production. Each is described in more detail below.

STAGES OF EVALUATION

FORMATIVE EVALUATIONS

You conduct formative evaluations during the Design, and Development and Testing Stages of any education materials project. You involve individuals from a target population and the client in making decisions that will influence the product design. When implemented, these decisions are further evaluated and validated. The information you gather during the evaluation is important because it focuses on acceptance by the learners who are the intended users of the product. Formative evaluation's primary goal is to ensure the e-learning product appeals to and will be used by a specific group of learners.

Other outcomes achieved through formative evaluation include:

- Communicating progress in the design and development to everyone involved in the project.
- Obtaining buy-in from the stakeholders.
- Identifying the most appropriate images, sounds, voices, etc., for use in the software.
- Minimizing rework that results from a failure to please or communicate.
- Ensuring a complete and functional program.
- Achieving the most effective results possible.

A common problem during formative evaluations is that attention gets directed to pleasing the client. Formative evaluation activities should ensure that *both the client and the learners* have had adequate input into the functionality, look and feel of the product. After all, the learners will be the ones interacting with the software, not the client.

You can use various techniques to gather formative data. These techniques include:

- SMEs and key clients review of all design documents.
- Focus groups evaluate assets, such as images, screen designs, sound effects and narrators' voices.

■ Representatives of the learning group and key clients participate in pilot testing of design strategies. This includes examining the navigation, content presentation, practice and assessment.

SUMMATIVE EVALUATIONS

Summative evaluations are conducted as a product moves from development to use. They involve members of your development team, the intended audience of users, and evaluation experts. There are two main reasons for conducting summative evaluations:

1. To determine if the development team completed their tasks successfully. (Is the final product error-free? Does it save appropriate records? Does it otherwise function as it was intended?)

2. To determine the effectiveness of the final product. (Does it teach what was intended? Is it as good as, or better than, other training methods you have used? Does it require the anticipated time to complete it?)

Early determination of what data needs to be collected by the Learning Management Systems (LMS), and how your organization will use the data, is extremely helpful at the summative evaluation stage. For example, each learner's time spent in training, his or her performance data, and other information may not be tracked to the detail you require, unless decisions about these evaluation activities are made early in the process. Additionally, when you plan ahead, you may be able to build features into the software that will automate much of the data collection and analysis. This will save you significant time in the long run.

I recommend that you use a third-party evaluator, someone who is not involved in the e-learning design and development, to conduct the evaluation. Their distance from the project adds credibility by communicating that an impartial and unbiased evaluation is being conducted. This can have multiple pay-offs down the road. It is especially helpful when you are discussing the value of your e-learning or trying to market it to others.

The findings from the summative evaluations can be extremely valuable to your organization. You might use them in marketing efforts because the numbers illustrate the benefits e-learning has to offer employees. Similarly, you can use the findings to promote the success of your e-learning initiative with upper management.

Regrettably, while there are many potential benefits from summative evaluations, most organizations do not conduct them. In an effort to save time and money, both accuracy and effectiveness are simply assumed by many organizations. Only when problems arise do they realize their attempt to cut costs has actually increased them.

MAINTENANCE EVALUATIONS

Maintenance evaluations ensure your training continues to meet the on-going needs of your organization.

These evaluations are conducted by your internal training staff during the Implementation, and Revising or Retiring Stages.

A formal maintenance evaluation should be established soon after the product goes live. After that, the frequency of your evaluations depends upon volatility of the content, your corporate environment, your hiring practices, and societal changes. As a general rule, it is better to review the software too often.

As we discussed earlier, both subtle and dramatic changes can reduce the effectiveness of your e-learning program. Maybe you will identify a change in the specific content your training should cover. It might be that you notice a change in the aesthetic preferences of your learners. Perhaps you will observe changes in the qualifications of the trainees coming into the organization. Any of these could mean that the basic assumptions originally used to design the training are no longer valid and revisions are called for.

Members of your client team typically conduct maintenance evaluations. SMEs periodically check to see that the training content is still accurate and appropriate. Meanwhile, training staff members are responsible for monitoring learners' needs and judging the aesthetic aspects of the program as times change.

PROCESS EVALUATIONS

At various points during the lifecycle of most e-learning products, there are some rough spots—times when things didn't work as well as everyone had hoped. Process evaluations are the answer to this predicament. The purpose of the process evaluation is to help you identify, analyze and eliminate problems so that the next e-learning project will run more smoothly. Specifically, the goal is to help you identify changes to the design and development process that will result in more effective, less expensive, and more quickly produced e-learning on future projects. Process evaluations shift the focus from the quality of the e-learning product onto the quality of the e-learning production process.

An effective process evaluation is dependent upon several factors:

- Complete and detailed records of your development process. Records will reveal the time, effort and cost associated with every aspect of the project. This will help in the identification of areas for improvement.
- The involvement of your entire e-learning team. The candid participation of the entire team is needed to provide explanation in support of the records. Individuals can provide the details that give added meaning to the numbers. They will help to determine if a problem was process-related and how it can be avoided in the future.
- Candid and open discussions about issues related to the project. This must include everyone from your entire e-learning design and development team, as well as any third-party vendors you worked with to create the e-learning. This will help you distinguish between process problems and issues related to personalities or skill levels.

For the process evaluation to be more than a project debriefing, four significant things must happen:

1. At the start of the project, everyone must understand the process will be evaluated, and they are responsible for supporting the data collection needed for it.
2. Detailed records, including an issues log, must be maintained throughout the project. This documentation will focus the evaluation.
3. Team members must know they have the protection they need to speak candidly about issues without fear of retribution.
4. The organization must act on the findings to improve the process. Otherwise future process evaluations will be viewed as meaningless activities.

When these things happen, there is tremendous growth and educational potential within your organization. You will observe that your e-learning team will grow stronger, and that your programs will improve.

14

Management
Systems

- Knowledge Management Systems (KMS)
- Learning Content Management Systems (LCMS)
- Learning Management Systems (LMS)

A virtual explosion of management systems has resulted from our reliance upon computers in the workplace: Human Resource Management Systems (HRMS) store and manipulate the growing volume of data collected on employees; and Inventory Management Systems (IMS) help retail organizations optimize the ordering, warehousing, display, sale and replenishment of the products they sell. Not surprisingly, several specialized forms of management systems have been developed that are closely associated with e-learning. In this chapter, I will discuss several of them: Knowledge Management Systems (KMS), Learning Content Management Systems (LCMS) and Learning Management Systems (LMS).

KNOWLEDGE MANAGEMENT SYSTEMS

Knowledge Management Systems (KMS) are designed to bring order to the overwhelming, and continuously expanding, volume of information produced by an organization. A KMS is the modern equivalent to a skilled long-term employee. In the past when someone in an organization needed to find a document, slide or videotape that hadn't been seen for a while, he or she might say, "Go ask Betty, she'll know where to find a copy of it." Now, the KMS fulfills that role.

A KMS provides a repository and retrieval mechanism for all forms of corporate or institutional documentation: reports, manuals, diagrams, animations, videos, photographs, audio recordings and anything else that can be digitized for storage. The KMS is, in effect, a large multimedia database. Items within the KMS are stored, categorized, identified by keywords, and systematized for optimal management and retrieval. The key to an effective KMS is entering (populating) data, and organizing it *effectively*. Ineffective use of the KMS, as with any management system, results in the "garbage in, garbage out" phenomena.

If an organization has done a good job populating the KMS, the following is an example of how it could be used:

> A training manager, Juan, just learned that he will offer a day-long course on the XLS series of tools in three weeks. To get a quick start on the development of a high-quality course, Juan conducts a search of the KMS for all information related to the XLS series. The search results in technical documents, a short video shipped with the product, photographs produced by the marketing department, a few documents outlining the competitive advantages of the series, a slideshow detailing the product features, and a short Web-based lesson on selling the series to existing customers. After viewing selected items, Juan quickly chooses several items that will serve as a foundation for his overview course and downloads them to his computer.

Juan realizes information in the KMS must be current to be effective. Everyone creating knowledge resources has to be responsible and see that they are properly input into the system. He knows the information he downloaded will save him time and effort. He plans to upload his presentation into the KMS when he has finished. Perhaps someone else in the organization will find his presentation a valuable resource in the future.

Although the KMS stores all the training documents for your organization, it is not appropriate to tell a group of employees to go to the KMS and learn about the XLS by themselves. Why? This approach requires employees to determine what is important to study, how long they should spend studying a document, and whether or not they have learned what they need to know. These are decisions most learners are not skilled at making. Furthermore, it offers little or no documentation of their effort or the knowledge they have gained.

LEARNING CONTENT MANAGEMENT SYSTEMS

Learning Content Management Systems (LCMS) are specialized forms of KMS. Like the KMS, the LCMS is basically a database. It manages all of an organizations documents related to education and training. In addition to specializing on education and training content, LCMS often support the use of learning objects (chapter 2). More advanced LCMS allow users to combine selected documents, or learning objects, into a sequence for presentation. In effect, the LCMS allows users to create a course from the various content components they identify.

Effective use of an LCMS requires rigid standards governing the design of the information modules included in the system. These standards ensure that a sequence of content modules appears to be a thoughtfully constructed whole, rather than a collection of disparate elements of information. Standards governing the elements entered into the LCMS must address all aspects of lesson design. They must cover the structure and statement of goals and objectives, navigation conventions, graphic treatments, audio levels, video formats, data collection, performance tracking and management, reporting requirement, and learner characteristics, such as skills, knowledge, age and gender, that may influence component design and, therefore, use. Without careful design guidance and compliance during development, an organization may end up with little more than a collection of brief lessons that are ill-suited for combination and reuse.

LEARNING MANAGEMENT SYSTEMS

Learning Management Systems (LMS) do just what their name implies: manage learning. While an LMS is an online tool, most systems manage a wide range of learning formats, including both online (CD-ROM, Web-based, digital video, etc.) and offline (videotapes, self-study booklets, seminars, etc.). The basic functions of an LMS are to organize learning materials, facilitate access to lessons, and track performance data for the benefit of both the organization and the learner.

There are many different LMS on the market today. Each offers a set of features and functions that its developers hope gives it the competitive advantage to make it an industry leader. However, all LMS have certain common features. Those defining features fall into three categories:

- Listing courses
- Associating learners with courses
- Administrative Functions: tracking and reporting performance data

I briefly discuss each category in the following paragraphs.

Listing Courses

As stated above, LMS do not simply manage e-learning, they manage all forms of education and training. As an organization begins to use an LMS, it populates it with existing courses and training materials. Usually, this process helps the organization to identify areas where it needs additional training resources. Some LMS list courses by title or the topic addressed in the instruction. Others attempt to identify specific objectives met by a course, and list those outcomes, and associate them back to the course. Each approach has its advantages, and one may be more appropriate than another in certain situations.

Associating Learners with Courses

Perhaps the most valuable feature of the LMS is that it gives learners *direct access* to the specific courses they must complete for their jobs. In order to accomplish this task effectively, each user must have a unique User ID recognizable to the LMS. The ID is generally associated with a job classification, and it is specifically associated with the user's individual records.

When an individual logs on to a LMS, he or she uses the User ID to access a record that shows the courses assigned to that person. This record also shows the status of the learner's courses (not accessed, begun or completed) as well as the nature of the course (e-learning, seminar, self-study, video, etc.). If the course materials assigned to this person need to be ordered, the LMS can process the order. If a learner must attend a seminar, the LMS often handles everything, from seminar registration to reserving a hotel room.

Tracking and Reporting Performance Data

Another huge benefit of an LMS is its automation of performance tracking and reporting. The LMS accomplishes this by linking to other enterprise systems, such as employee databases and Human Resources Management Systems (HRMS). By periodically uploading a current employee database, the LMS will be able manage the learning of all current employees. By linking to the HRMS, the LMS can automatically update performance data and compliance records as employees complete learning modules.

Installing the LMS, integrating it with other enterprise systems, and populating its database with courses can be a daunting task. For this reason, many organizations initially implement the LMS on a limited basis and expand, or "scale-up," the implementation as needed.

15

Determining the *Value* of e-Learning

Cost/Benefit Analysis ▪

Return on Investment (ROI) Analysis ▪

W hat is the value of e-learning for your organization? That is a tough question to answer. Determining the true value of your e-learning, as with any training program, can be a time-intensive challenge. The most commonly discussed approach is calculating a return on investment (ROI). A less frequently discussed, but often used, technique is a cost/benefit analysis. Both approaches have their strengths and weaknesses when it comes to determining the value of e-learning.

COST/BENEFIT ANALYSIS

When you conduct a cost/benefit analysis, you generally compare the cost of e-learning development and delivery with that of an alternative form of training. This may, on the surface, appear to be a simple and straightforward calculation. In reality, it can become quite complex. And, it is important to realize that the accuracy of your calculations is directly related to the effort put into them.

To determine cost/benefit, first estimate development cost for both e-learning and the training mode it will replace. You do this by multiplying the hours of training your team needs developed by an average development cost-per-hour. For a one-day seminar, with eight hours of training at a cost of $6,000 per hour, it would cost you $48,000. Remember, as you estimate the cost of e-learning, that e-learning training time, when compared to traditional training, typically ranges from 30% to 70% less. Therefore, an e-learning program covering the same content might take only four hours for your employees to complete, instead of eight. A four-hour e-learning seminar, with a development cost of $35,000 per hour, would cost you $140,000.

Now, compare the development costs for the two approaches. If you are only training 50 employees, and they all work at the same facility, your decision at this point should be clear—offer a seminar.

But, let's look at a scenario that is more typical for organizations that are considering the use of e-learning. What if you are training 400 employees, and they are located across the country or around the world? Now, the *delivery cost* becomes an important consideration.

Determining your delivery cost can be a complex proposition. Generally, this involves calculating wages, benefits, expenses, and lost opportunity costs:

- Wages and benefits paid to everyone while traveling to and participating in the training.
- Travel expenses for the trainers and trainees. This includes transportation, per diem, lodging, car rentals, etc.
- Publishing and shipping training materials.
- The lost productivity or opportunity costs that you incur when your staff is away from work to participate in the training.

After calculating the full delivery costs for both the seminar training and e-learning approaches, you will likely find e-learning is hundreds of thousands of dollars less expensive to deliver. This clearly shifts the financial benefit back to e-learning. Of course, this e-learning scenario assumes the infrastructure for your organization to deliver e-learning is already in place.

RETURN ON INVESTMENT ANALYSIS (ROI)

Return on investment (ROI) calculations extend beyond those of a cost/benefit analysis. ROI calculations look at the financial benefit generated as a *result of the training*, not just the savings. ROI goes so far as to ask:

- Have our sales increased as a result of the training?
- Has the training decreased overhead expenses, such as facility, legal, healthcare, benefits, and recruitment and retention costs?
- Has our organization realized a financial benefit that can be attributed to the training?

The complexity of the questions you ask is one reason why conducting an ROI analysis is so complex. Extensive pre-intervention baseline data must be available for you to compare with post e-learning findings. These data need to be gathered from existing statistics on sales, profit margin, training, expenses associated with topics covered in your training (such as injury or legal defense), and other areas that may be affected by learning outcomes.

One complicating factor in ROI analysis is *time*: Time must be permitted to pass before you take measurements for your comparison with the baseline data. You must determine when sufficient time elapses before you measure the effects of your training. However, as time is passing, many events will occur that may affect your findings. For example, your organization may decide to refocus its efforts, a new government administration that is favorable to your industry takes office, or a global economic reversal occurs and your sales efforts are thwarted. Any of these things could affect the numbers—and how you interpret them.

Regardless of the method you select for determining the value of an e-learning program, there are two categories of questions you should consider:

■ Outcomes and
■ Advantages

Questions you should ask related to e-learning *outcomes* include the following:

■ Do users learn what they need to know?
■ Do users find e-learning to be an effective approach to training?
■ Do users spend less time in training than they did with traditional approaches?
■ Can users easily transfer what they learn to the workplace?

Questions related to advantages derived from e-learning include the following:

- Does your organization enjoy an improved status as a result of e-learning?
- Does your organization enjoy a stronger position in the market as a result of e-learning?
- Has e-learning had a positive impact on attitudes or morale?
- Does your organization find it easier to recruit and retain employees?

The answers to these questions will show you the real value of your e-learning. They provide you with the facts you need to communicate the true return your organization receives from its investment in an e-learning initiative.

As with the other topics in this book, calculating cost/benefit and ROI may seem unduly complex and demanding. But, just as with the other topics I covered, my decades of work in this area have convinced me that the quality of the product is directly related to the effort put into producing it.

I am confident that by using this quick guide you will experience a successful e-learning initiative in your organization. I wish you the best of luck.

Notes